OXFORD
UNIVERSITY PRESS

Maya's Family

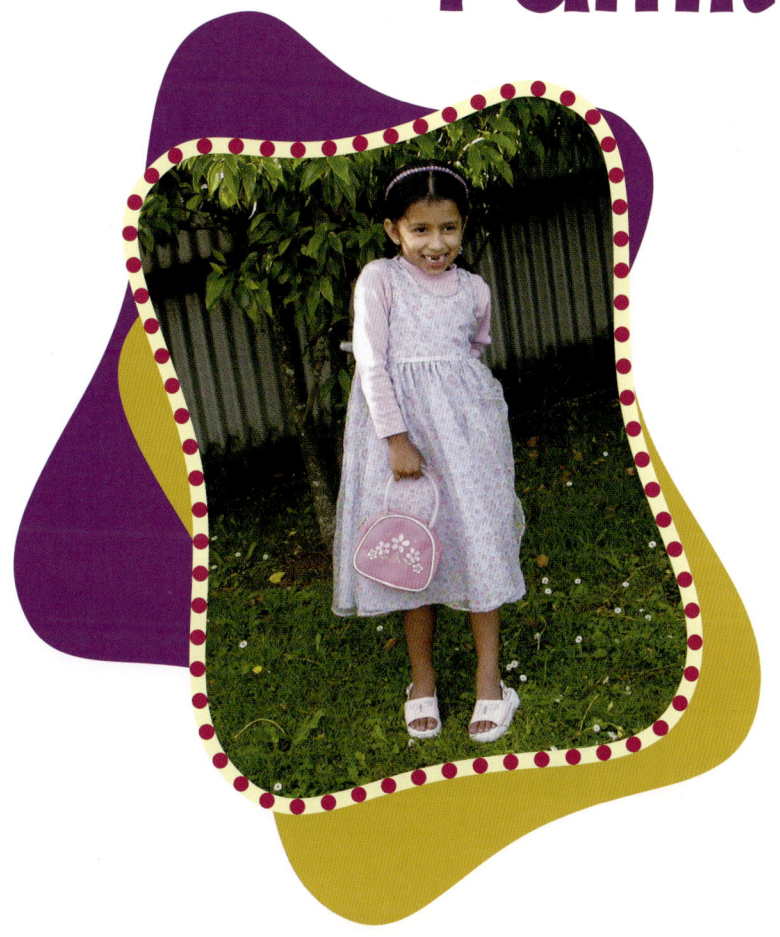

Luther Reimer

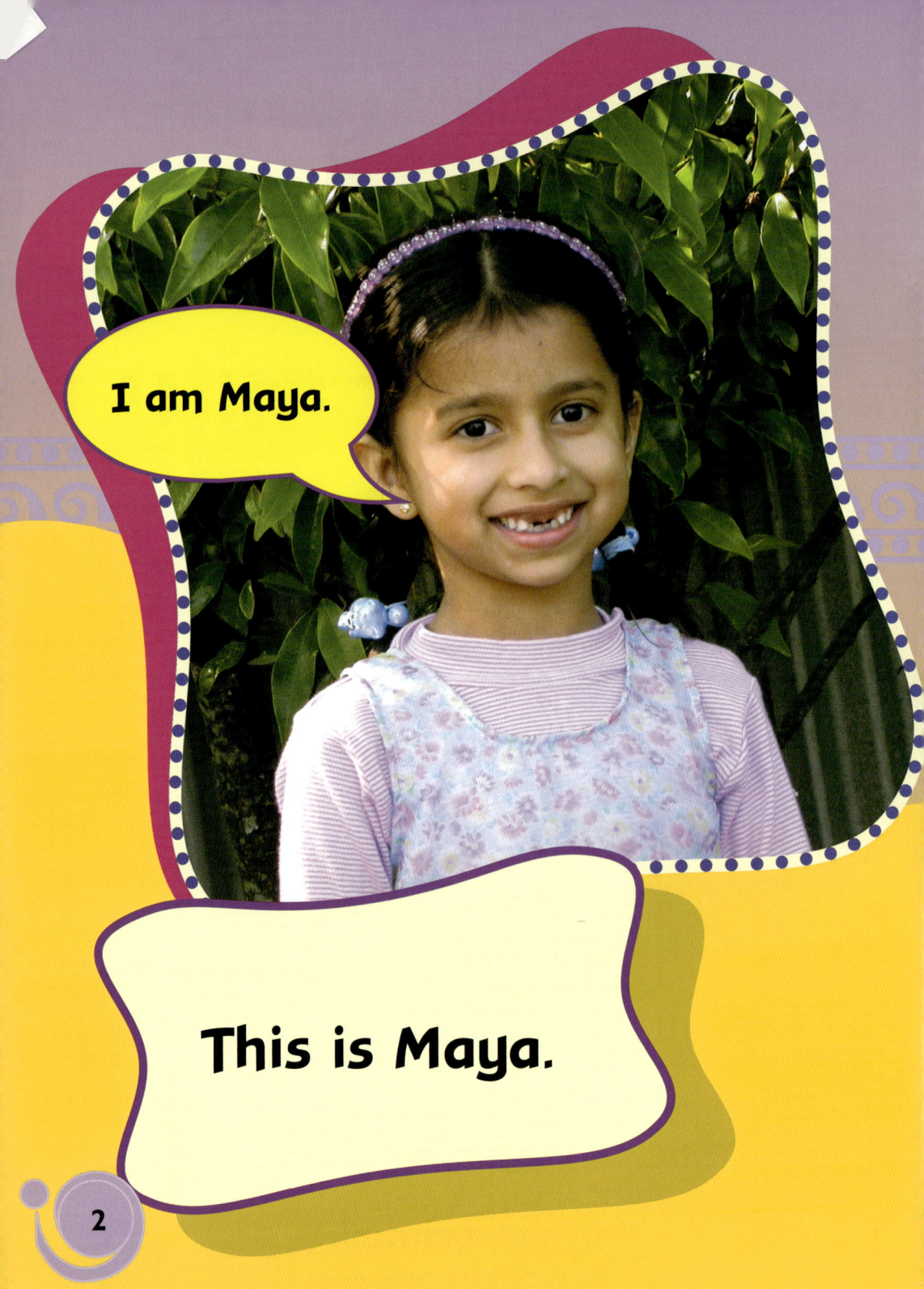

I am Maya.

This is Maya.

2

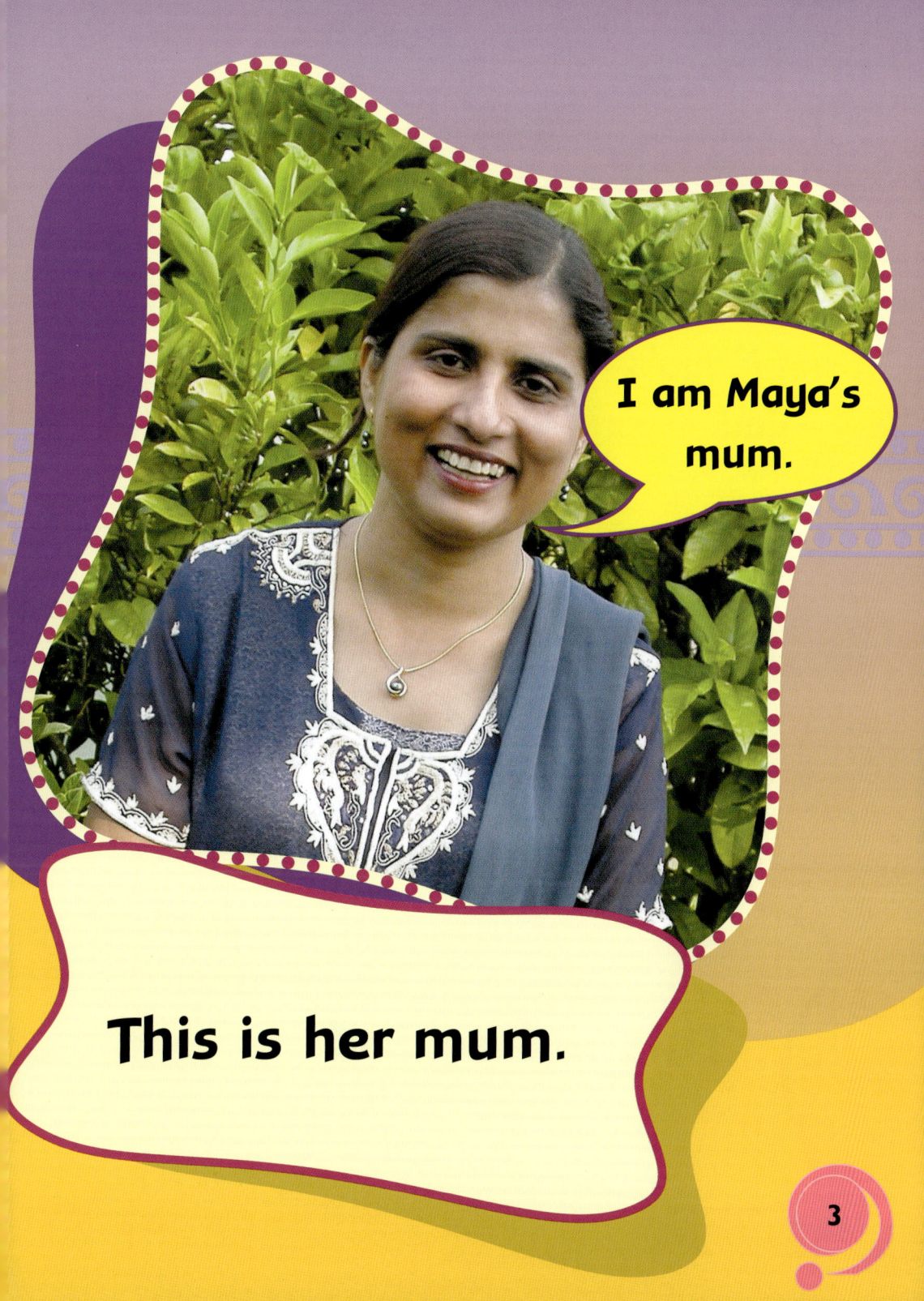

I am Maya's mum.

This is her mum.

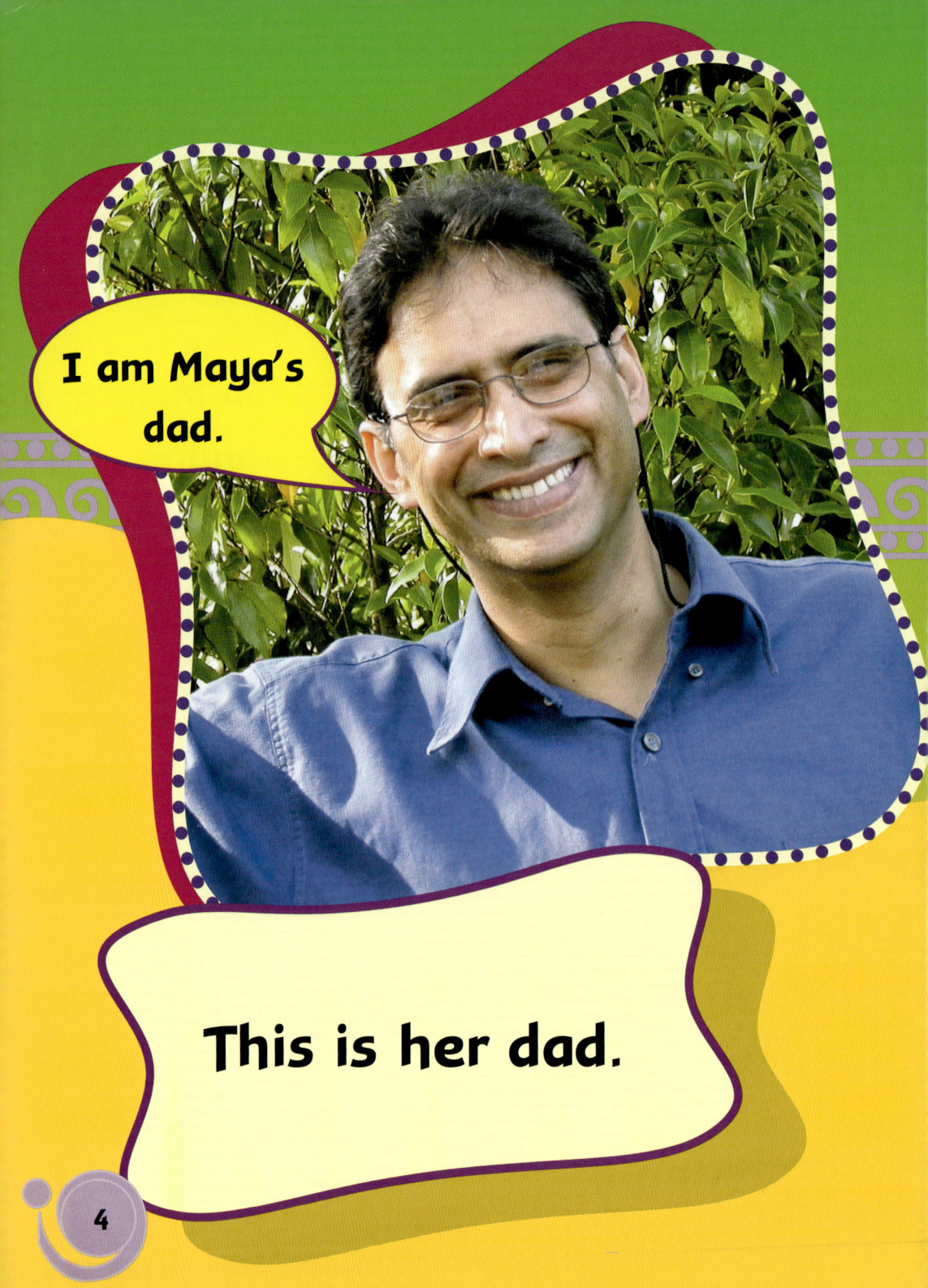

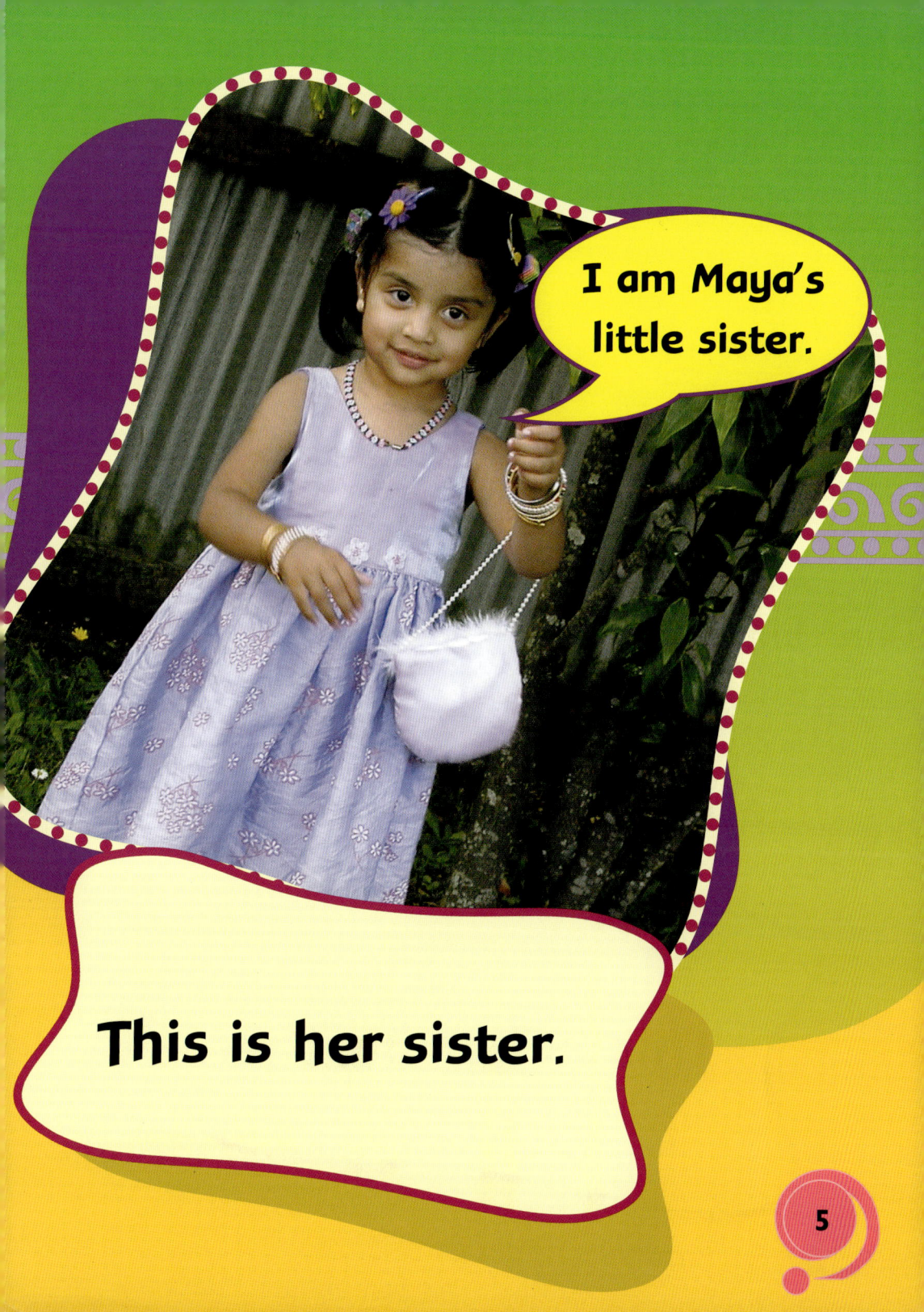

This is her sister.

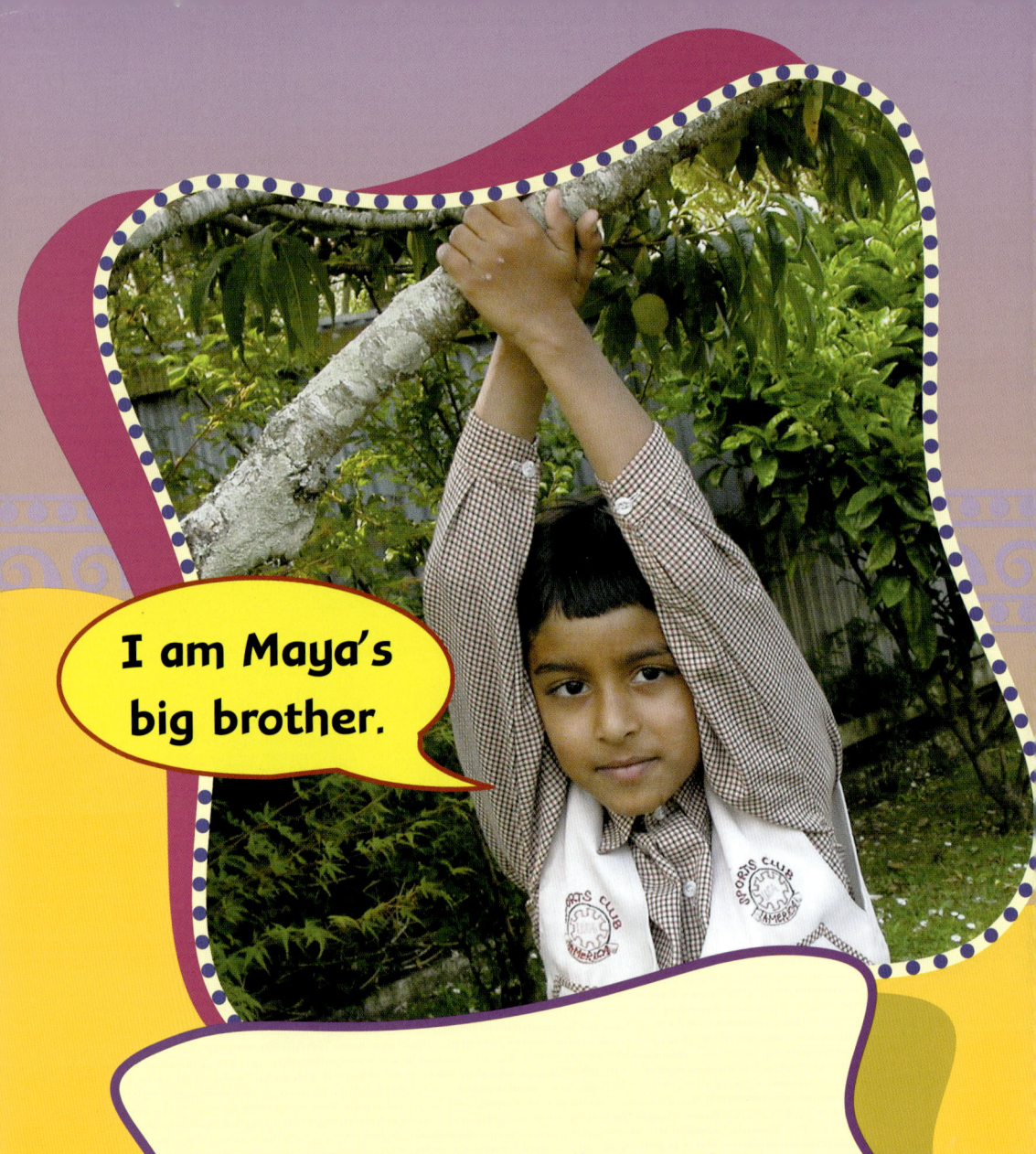

I am Maya's big brother.

This is her brother.

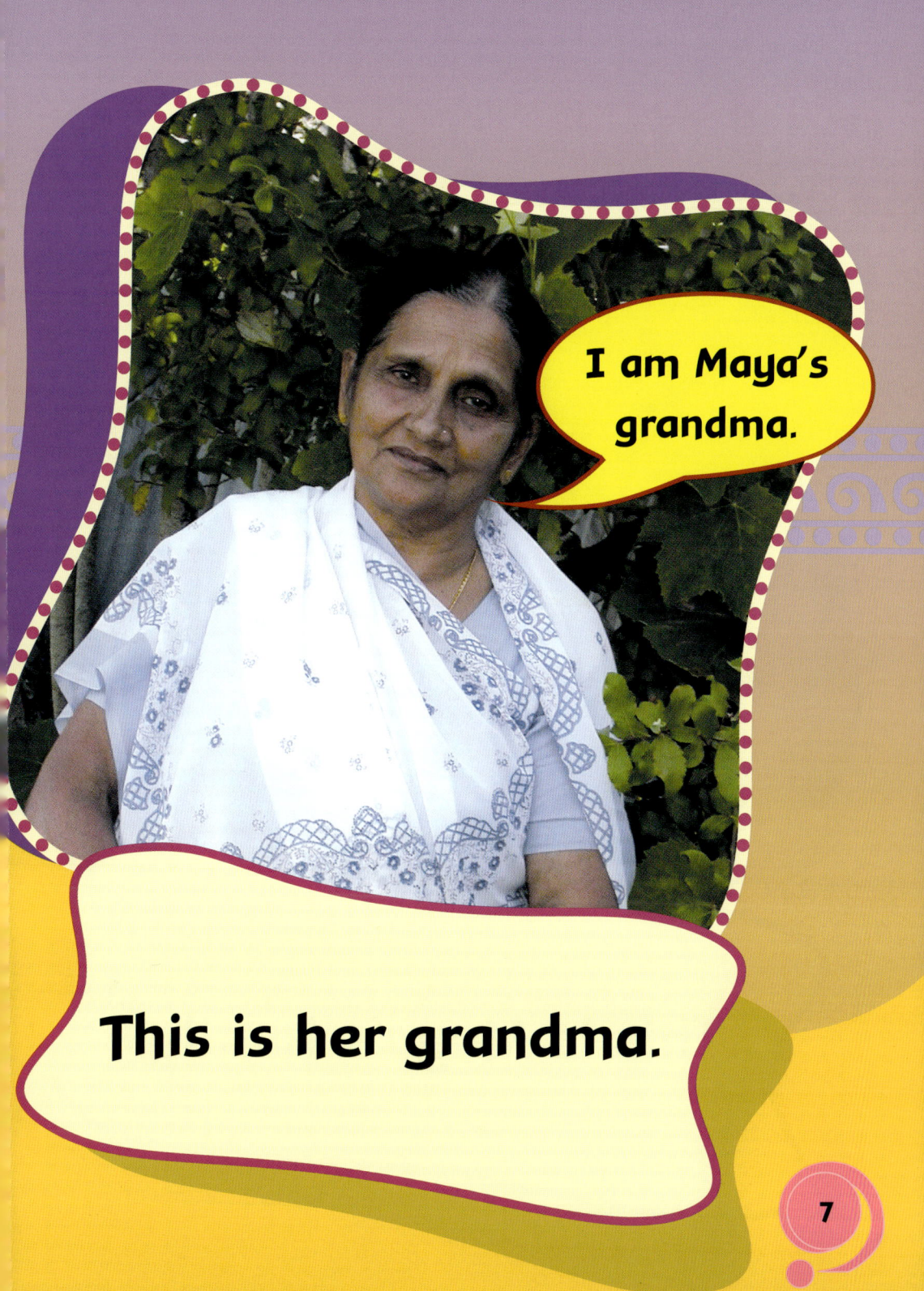

I am Maya's grandma.

This is her grandma.

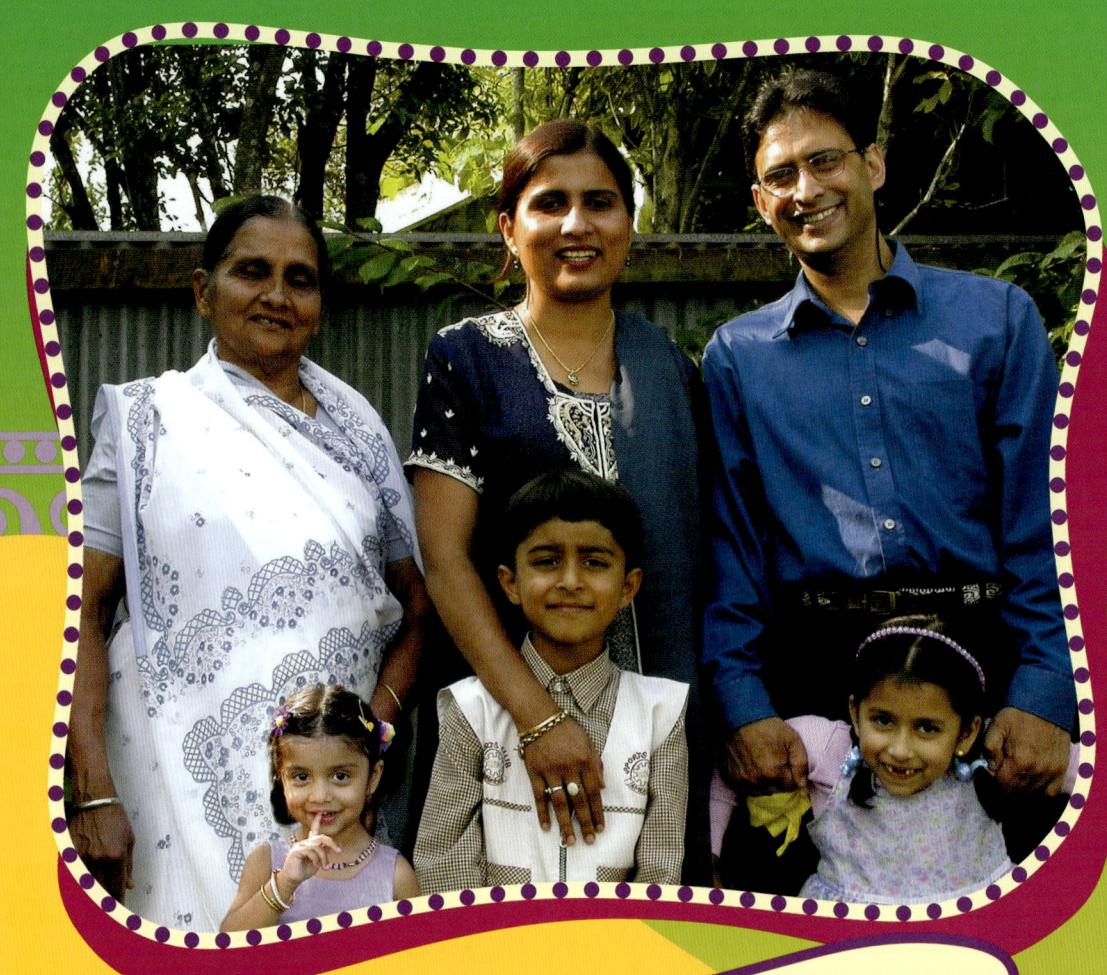

This is Maya's family.